# CHEETAHS

LIVING WILD

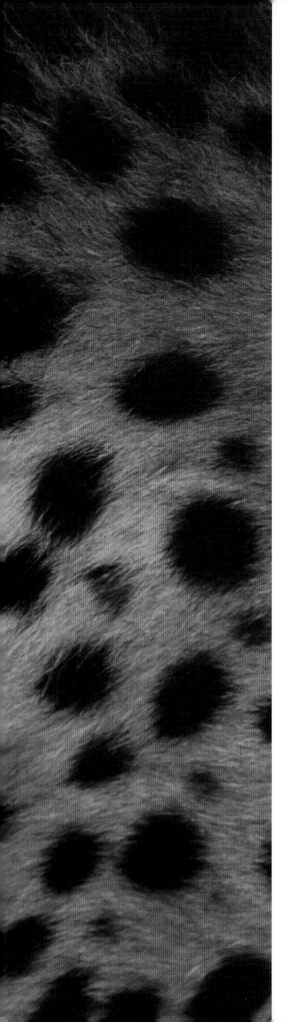

# LIVING WILD

Published by Creative Education
P.O. Box 227, Mankato, Minnesota 56002
Creative Education is an imprint of The Creative Company
www.thecreativecompany.us

Design and production by Mary Herrmann
Art direction by Rita Marshall
Printed in the United States of America

Photographs by 123RF (Ablestock Premium), Alamy (Luke MacGregor, Andy Rouse-Wildlife, Ann and Steve Toon), AP Images, Corbis (Eddi Boehnke/zefa, DLILLC, Gallo Images, Martin Harvey/Gallo Images, Frans Lanting, Lynda Richardson, Paul A. Souders), Dreamstime (Ankimo, Bucky_za, Ecophoto, Kitch, Nightowiza, Rgbe, Stephenmeese, Xtremesafari), Getty Images (Martin Harvey, Indian School, Michael K. Nichols), iStockphoto (Mark Atkins, Gez Browning, Eric Gevaert, David T. Gomez, Kaido Kärner, Hilton Kotze, Peter Malsbury, Graeme Purdy, Hansjoerg Richter, Ana Schechter, Michael Sheehan, Victor Soares)

The poem on page 35 first appeared in *The Orphan Calf and the Magical Cheetah: Cheetah Poems, Essays, and Illustrations by the Namibian People*, published in 1996 by the Cheetah Conservation Fund. Reprinted by permission of the CCF.

Library of Congress Cataloging-in-Publication Data
Hanel, Rachael.
Cheetahs / by Rachael Hanel.
p. cm. — (Living wild)
Includes bibliographical references and index.
ISBN 978-1-58341-737-9
1. Cheetah—Juvenile literature. I. Title. II. Series.

QL737.C23H3517 2009
599.75'9—dc22    2008009500

First Edition
9 8 7 6 5 4 3 2 1

**¢ CREATIVE EDUCATION**

# CHEETAHS

Rachael Hanel

The sun shines bright and hot on the African savanna. A group of gazelles rests around a watering hole.

The gazelles do not know it yet,
but they are being hunted.

The sun shines bright and hot on the African **savanna**. A group of gazelles rests around a watering hole. They graze on grass and take long drinks of water. The gazelles do not know it yet, but they are being hunted. Several hundred yards away, a hungry cheetah fixes its eyes upon the herd. The cheetah slinks closer to the group, staying in plain sight. Because of its incredible speed, the cheetah does not need to rely upon the element of surprise. Every

animal in the herd now sees the cheetah. The gazelles stop what they are doing and stare. The cheetah stares back, still inching forward. When the cheetah is about 200 feet (61 m) away, it launches into a sprint, scattering the herd. The cheetah zeroes in on a young and slow gazelle. With one swipe of its paw, the cheetah knocks down its prey. It has secured a meal for another day.

# WHERE IN THE WORLD THEY LIVE

☐ **African Cheetah**
Namibia,
Botswana, South
Africa, Kenya,
Tanzania, and
other countries
throughout
southern Africa

☐ **Northwest African
Cheetah**
North Africa
and parts of
western Africa

**Asiatic Cheetah**
Iran

Most of the world's cheetahs live
in parts of southern, eastern, and
central Africa and are known
collectively as African cheetahs.
However, two endangered
subspecies known as the northwest
African cheetah and the Asiatic
cheetah can also be found in
the region of North Africa and
the country of Iran respectively.
The colored squares on the map
represent the three cheetahs'
largest home regions.

## INCREDIBLE SPEED

The agile cheetah is the fastest animal on Earth. Its speed and spotted fur make it one of the most distinctive animals to roam the African plains. The cheetah is a member of the Felidae family, which includes lions, tigers, leopards, and the domestic house cat. The cheetah looks most like a leopard, but the spots of both animals are different, and the two cats behave much differently, too.

The cheetah's scientific species name is *Acinonyx jubatus*. *Acinonyx* is Greek for "thorn claw," and in Latin, *jubatus* means "maned." The word "cheetah" comes from the Hindi language, which is spoken in India. There, Hindus called the animal *chita*, which means "spotted one."

All cheetahs' fur is covered with distinctive dark spots, and no two cheetahs have the same set of markings. The spots measure about .75 to 1.25 inches (2–3.2 cm) around. On the tail, the spots merge to form four to six rings. A white **tuft** marks the end of the tail, and the belly is also white. The mostly black and tan

In the wild, cheetah cubs are vulnerable to attack by lions and hyenas and have only a 50 percent chance of survival.

fur provides effective **camouflage** for cheetahs in tall savanna grasses.

From a distance, a cheetah's fur appears soft, but in actuality, it is coarse and wiry. The fur of the spots is slightly longer and softer than the tan fur. The tan fur forms a small ridge on the back of the neck, like a mane. This mane is usually more prominent in male cheetahs, but it is not as large as a lion's mane. Long, black lines of fur, called tear lines, run down each side of a cheetah's nose. Some scientists think that the tear lines reduce the glare of the strong African sun, protecting the cheetah's eyes.

Male and female cheetahs share many physical characteristics. Both have small heads and ears in relation to their bodies. However, males are larger than females. An adult male can weigh up to 140 pounds (64 kg), while a female weighs around 90 pounds (41 kg). Cheetahs stand about 30 inches (76 cm) tall at the shoulder. From head to rump, a fully grown cheetah is about four feet (1.2 m) long, with the tail measuring about half of that length.

Both inside and out, almost every part of a cheetah's body is built for speed. A cheetah can run up to 70 miles

*Naturally fast animals, cheetahs are known primarily for their ability to run at great speeds.*

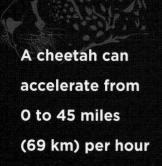

**A cheetah can accelerate from 0 to 45 miles (69 km) per hour in only 2 seconds.**

(121 km) per hour—a speed without comparison in the world of land animals. A cheetah's spine sets its quickness in motion. Before it runs, a cheetah rounds its back to warm up the spine and extends its front legs, crossing its paws. Then it releases the arch like a wound-up spring and bolts into a sprint. Indeed, the cheetah's spine functions much like a spring, as it has the ability to expand and contract.

To run at top speed, a cheetah extends its lean, powerful legs. Its legs are longer and leaner than those of other cats. The cheetah runs on its toes with the help of its claws, which are long and rounded. A cheetah cannot **retract** its claws. For this reason, its paws look more like a dog's than a cat's. As the animal sprints, its claws dig into the ground, providing traction, much like cleats on shoes. The traction, coupled with the heavily muscled tail, prevents the cheetah from tipping over while changing direction at high speeds. A cheetah can cover up to 20 feet (6 m) in one stride and take 3 strides per second. For a split second during its stride, all four legs lift off the ground.

Even a cheetah's respiratory system helps it run quickly. A cheetah's chest is large to make room for sizable lungs that can hold more oxygen than the lungs of other cats. At its top speed of 70 miles (121 km) per hour, a cheetah takes 150 breaths per minute. Its strong heart and wide arteries allow the maximum amount of blood to flow and supply oxygen to hard-working muscles. A cheetah's wide nostrils and sinus cavities allow it to breathe in more oxygen than other cats can.

But cheetahs are not endurance athletes. They can sustain high speeds for only brief distances before they tire. After only 400 to 600 yards (366–550 m), a cheetah's body temperature rises from its normal temperature of 102 °F (39 °C) to 105 °F (41 °C). Remaining at this higher temperature can be fatal, so a cheetah stops running and pants to cool off. After a sprint, it can take up to 20 minutes for the cat to regain the energy needed to sprint again.

A cheetah's speed and sharp senses make it an effective hunter. Cheetahs possess a strong sense of smell and excellent eyesight. A cheetah can spot prey from up to three miles (5 km) away. The eyes, located at the very front of the head, help a cheetah accurately judge distance. A **retina** in the eye that is longer than other

*Because cheetahs are active during the heat of the day, they conserve their energy when stalking prey.*

*An annoyed cheetah cub will show its displeasure by growling, hissing, and spitting.*

A cheetah does not need much time to chase and kill its prey. The entire process can take as little as 20 seconds.

felines' retinas gives a cheetah a wide-angle view of its surroundings.

A cheetah's teeth are smaller than those of other big cats because its large nasal passages don't leave as much room for the roots of teeth to grow. Rather than killing an animal such as a gazelle with a bite, a cheetah will suffocate its prey using its strong jaws. A cheetah's teeth may be small, but they are sharp. **Incisors** help it scrape the meat off bone. Jagged **molars** allow the cheetah to grind flesh into smaller pieces. Cheetahs have 30 teeth, with 15 on each side of the mouth. The animal's tongue is covered with tiny hooks called rasps. The rasps allow the cheetah to remove dirt and burrs from its fur. The rough tongue also helps scrape flesh off bone.

There are about 12,000 to 15,000 cheetahs living in the wild today. They live mostly on the African savanna, surrounded by tall grasses, some trees, and mounds of dirt. The largest cheetah populations are found in southern Africa in the countries of Namibia and Botswana, in Kenya and Tanzania in eastern Africa, and in some parts of northwestern Africa. An estimated 100 Asiatic cheetahs live in the Middle Eastern country of Iran.

Males usually live together in groups separate from females, with the males establishing a set territory.

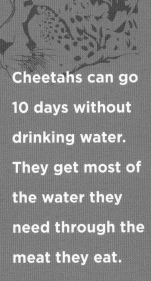

**Cheetahs can go 10 days without drinking water. They get most of the water they need through the meat they eat.**

A cheetah may roam the savanna by itself. But often, the animals will form small groups that hunt and live together. A group of cheetahs may consist of a few related males, which is called a coalition. Another common unit is made up of a mother and her cubs.

Cheetahs are not highly territorial because they are usually spaced far enough apart. The size of a cheetah's territory varies widely and depends upon the amount of prey within it. Territories can be as small as 40 square miles (104 sq km) or, in rare cases, as large as 800 square miles (2,070 sq km).

Cheetahs spend most of their days resting in order to conserve energy for hunting. A cheetah also devotes much of its time to cleaning itself with its tongue. Sometimes cheetahs will pair up and lick each other. Temperatures on the African plains average 78 to 86 °F (25 to 30 °C) in the summer, so during the heat of the day, cheetahs find a cool place to rest, such as under a tree. They typically hunt in either early morning or late afternoon.

An adult cheetah needs to eat an average of six pounds (2.7 kg) of meat per day to survive. A large meal (above) will satisfy a cheetah for several days.

Cheetahs dine on antelopes, gazelles, hares, birds, and warthogs. Hunting in a group makes it easier to find food, and a coalition may work together to kill larger animals such as buffalo and wildebeest. To spot prey, a cheetah will scan the savanna from a higher vantage point, such as a rock or low branch. Once it picks out its prey—usually the most vulnerable member of a herd—the cheetah begins to move closer to it while staying low to the ground. With about 200 feet (61 m) to go, the cheetah launches into a sprint. Because a cheetah can sustain its high speed for only short bursts, the prey often escapes; a cheetah is successful on only about half of its hunts.

As it gets closer to its victim, a cheetah extends a paw to knock it down. A sharp **dewclaw** on the inside of the cheetah's paw sinks into the animal and helps to pull it over. Death comes when the cheetah clamps its jaws around the victim's neck. The cheetah drags the **carcass** to a secluded area, such as under a tree. After a kill, a cheetah is tired. It might rest for several minutes before it eats. When it is tired, it is no match for stronger predators such as lions and hyenas, which can easily snatch away its food. A cheetah kills an average of one animal every other day.

Male and female cheetahs can come together to mate at any time of the year. When a female is ready to mate, she enters a male's territory and releases a special scent in her urine. This scent attracts the male. The male approaches, but if the female isn't ready for his company, she swats at him and sends him away. He can get near her only when she's ready. They will stay together for a few

*Females live solitary lives, except when raising their cubs, and even that they do by themselves.*

*Cheetahs begin mating at around age three, and females can have many cubs in their short lifetimes.*

days. But after mating, the male leaves. He does not help to raise the young, called cubs.

Cubs are born about three months after the male and female mate. When she's ready to give birth, a female cheetah finds a quiet, isolated place in which to lie down. This may be a patch of tall grass, under a tree or shrub, or behind large rocks. She gives birth to a **litter** of between two and five cubs, though as many as eight can be born at once. Cubs are blind and tiny when they are born, weighing only 8 to 10 ounces (227–284 g) and measuring 9 inches (23 cm) long. They drink their mother's milk, and she licks them clean with her tongue. The repetitive stroking motion of her licking also helps them digest milk. Cubs communicate with their mothers by making a low, chirping sound that resembles a bird's call. A mother will move her cubs frequently to avoid predators such as hyenas or lions. She moves them one at a time, carrying them in her mouth by the scruffs of their necks.

Cheetahs have dark fur when they are born, and their spots are barely visible. They have a thick coat of gray fur, called a mantle, along their neck and back. The fur is about three inches (8 cm) long and makes the

**Like house cats, cheetahs purr when they are content. A cheetah's purr can be heard from 20 feet (6 m) away.**

cub appear bigger than it really is. The downy coat acts as camouflage, helping the cubs blend in with their surroundings. The mantle fur falls out after three to eight months, revealing the usual spotted cheetah fur.

Cubs open their eyes after 5 to 10 days and begin to crawl. They walk at three weeks and start to follow their mother at six weeks. At that time, they weigh about five and a half pounds (2.5 kg). Their teeth come in quickly, after just two weeks, and cubs start eating meat at four weeks old. The mother will then leave them alone to hunt for food that she can bring back to them. The cubs stay quiet and still while she is gone. Without their mother, they are more vulnerable to attack by predators. When the mother makes a kill, she lets the cubs eat first so they can grow fast. They will get their adult teeth after 10 to 14 months.

As cubs grow, their playful running and swatting at each other helps them practice for the day when they will run fast and have to knock down prey. At about seven months, they start to hunt with their mother. Cubs catch their own prey at about one year of age. By the time they are 16 to 18 months old, cheetahs can hunt

by themselves. At this time, the mother leaves them to mate again. While brothers may group together for life, female cheetahs will strike out on their own but settle close to their mother. A cheetah's life expectancy is between 7 and 12 years in the wild. In captivity, a cheetah can live between 12 and 17 years.

Male cubs are often forced to move far away from their mother's home range by older, more territorial males.

## A POPULATION IN DECLINE

*The swiftness of the cheetah (above) was admired by the ancient kings who kept them as pets (opposite).*

Evidence of relationships between cheetahs and humans extends back 5,000 years to the time of the ancient Egyptians. The Egyptians worshiped the animal as a cat-goddess, and pictures of cheetahs often decorated the tombs, or burial places, of wealthy Egyptians. In the nearby kingdom of Sumeria, located in present-day Iraq, images of cheetahs appeared on coins.

In 16th-century India, the ruler Akbar the Great kept detailed records of his 9,000 captive cheetahs. Akbar, along with other royalty throughout southern Asia who kept cheetahs, devised a hunting game for them called coursing. The sport, which drew large crowds of spectators, involved cheetahs being taken from their cages to the countryside. Hoods were put over their heads as they traveled. The prey were given a head start, then the hoods were removed from the cheetahs, and a race to catch the prey ensued. People were entertained by watching how quickly the cheetahs could track down their meal.

From the 11th through the 13th centuries, European **Crusaders** noted that Palestinians and Syrians in the Middle East used cheetahs to hunt gazelles. Later, wealthy

people in Renaissance Italy and France also used cheetahs as hunting companions from the 1500s through the 1700s.

It is estimated that by 1900, there were 100,000 cheetahs in 44 countries. Many of those animals had been removed from their natural habitats and kept in captivity throughout Europe and India. People soon learned that cheetahs kept in captivity do not breed well. By the late 1950s, the animal had disappeared from India and the Middle Eastern country of Israel.

The 20th century brought with it several blows to the worldwide cheetah population. For one, the human population in Africa increased significantly, and farms and ranches expanded into traditional cheetah territory. This **encroachment** disrupted the savanna habitat, and cheetahs' natural prey were driven away. Cheetahs then began to target domesticated farm animals such as cattle and sheep for food. Farmers were quick to kill cheetahs that they perceived as threats to their livestock.

During this time, hunters also prized cheetahs for their coats. In the 1960s, traders imported 1,500 cheetah pelts each year to the United States. By the 1970s, researchers noted the overall cheetah population numbered just

30,000. In 1974, the U.S. passed the Endangered Species Act, which made it illegal for people in the U.S. to keep cheetahs as pets. In 1975, the Convention on International Trade of Endangered Species (CITES) classified the cheetah as one of the most critically endangered animals on Earth. Because of this status, trade of live cheetahs or cheetah products has become illegal in most parts of the world. In addition, the International Union for Conservation of Nature Red List of Threatened Species

*Among the big cats, the long-legged cheetah is most closely related to the second-largest cat in the Americas, the cougar.*

*Cheetahs are protected in Botswana and South Africa's Kgalagadi Transfrontier Park, established in 2000.*

has categorized the cheetah as vulnerable since 1986.

Still, such protective measures did not result in the immediate reversal of the cheetah's decline. The population continued to decrease into the 1980s, when conflicts between humans and cheetahs peaked. From 1980 to 1991, an estimated 6,782 cheetahs were killed. Today, some countries allow a small number of cheetahs to be hunted each year. For example, in Namibia, 150 cheetahs can be killed each year, and 50 hunting licenses are issued in nearby Zimbabwe.

About one-tenth of the world's cheetahs currently live in captivity. However, cheetahs tend to breed less often when in captivity, and they are also more susceptible to disease. In 1982, a disease called feline infectious peritonitis killed more than half the cheetahs living at Wildlife Safari, an animal park in Winston, Oregon. Because of decreased reproduction rates and increased exposure to disease within captivity, the survival of the species depends on its survival in the wild.

Yet even those cheetahs that live in protected native environments face threats. Tourists who flock to wildlife reserves can disrupt the habits of cheetahs. Cheetahs hunt

**Some limited international trade in live cheetahs and their skins is still allowed in Namibia, Zimbabwe, and Botswana.**

*Cheetahs are allowed to hunt fast prey such as gazelles in Kenya's Masai Mara National Reserve.*

during the day, which is when most tourists ride through the reserves. This disruption can decrease a cheetah's success rate while hunting. In large game reserves, cheetahs are sometimes forced out by other predators such as lions and hyenas. Most cheetahs live outside of reserves, where they are not protected.

For thousands of years, people have admired the cheetah for its strength, speed, and agility. The first cheetah taken to a modern zoo was kept at London Zoo in 1829, but it did not live even a year. In 1871, New York City's Central

Park Zoo became the first in the U.S. to keep a cheetah.

Considering that the cheetah's appearance lends itself well to cartoonish representation, it is no wonder that the animal shows up often in popular culture. Perhaps one of the best-known cartoon cheetahs is Chester Cheetah. Chester Cheetah is the mascot for Cheetos, a cheesy corn chip. Chester Cheetah wears sunglasses and a black leather jacket. In commercials, he uses his quickness and stealth to try to grab Cheetos from unsuspecting snackers.

The 1980s television cartoon series *ThunderCats* featured

*The cheetah's often snarly appearance lends itself well to villainous representations of the animal.*

humans with feline characteristics. One of the characters was a female named Cheetara. She was the fastest of the ThunderCats and could quickly escape from enemies. She sported blonde hair with dark brown spots. After the show debuted, a toy line was launched, as well as comic books. In 2007, the film studio Warner Bros. announced a deal to turn *ThunderCats* into an animated movie.

In the Wonder Woman comics, a character named the Cheetah is Wonder Woman's archenemy. This character is the **alter ego** of Dr. Barbara Ann Minerva. According to the comic story, Minerva found a tribe in Africa whose female guardian had the powers of a cheetah. The guardian was killed, and Minerva asked a priest to instill her with the cheetah's powers.

Cheetahs have also starred in movies. *Duma* (2005) tells the story of a young South African boy whose family takes in an orphaned cheetah cub. As the cub grows, the boy realizes that he must return the animal to its native habitat before it becomes too tame to live in the wild. The boy and cheetah face many obstacles as they trek across the harsh African landscape to reach the savanna.

# A TEAR

From a distance there is a tear,
Receiving one, but stalking all.
The dark eye watches you from
Within the tall grasses.
Come closer,
The muscles become tense,
Suddenly there is dust of speed.
A strong body curved with strength
Gets his one.
As he lies with pride,
You will notice
The tear is a cry
For Survival.

*Cindy du Toit, from* The Orphan Calf
and the Magical Cheetah: Cheetah
Poems, Essays, and Illustrations by
the Namibian People

## CONSERVATION SCIENCE

Scientists think cheetahs may have **evolved** more than 20 million years ago, but many say that the animal first appeared in a form similar to today's cheetahs about 3.75 to 7.5 million years ago. These first cheetahs were larger than present-day ones and weighed about 200 pounds (91 kg). Fossil records also indicate that these cheetah ancestors may have originated in the southwestern and western U.S.

Between 2 million and 10,000 years ago, cheetahs moved from North America to the other continents. Cheetahs like those of today first appeared about 200,000 years ago in Africa and Europe. At that time, there were four species of cheetah. But at the end of the last great ice age, about 10,000 years ago, three of the four species—including those in North America and Europe—died out.

Because just one species has been breeding over the past 10,000 years, today's cheetahs exhibit signs of **inbreeding**. More than 99 percent of cheetahs' genes are the same. Because continuous inbreeding can result in weakened and sickly cheetahs, scientists have developed

**Even though cheetahs may perch in a low branch for a short time, they don't often climb trees like other cats do.**

A cheetah eats only what it kills, and the meat must be fresh. Cheetahs are not lured by hunters who leave food in traps.

a strategy called the Species Survival Plan (SSP) to help breed cheetahs that are as distantly related as possible. The plan contains the genetic codes and blood samples for captive cheetahs in North America. Each cheetah's parents, date of birth, and zoo location are listed. Female cheetahs in zoos are often artificially **inseminated** with sperm from wild cheetahs in Namibia. This ensures a larger genetic diversity among both captive cheetahs and those on wildlife reserves.

Up until the 1970s, it was rare that cheetah cubs were born in captivity. Today, thanks to the SSP, more and more cheetahs are reproducing successfully in zoos. The National Zoo in Washington, D.C., has created both a Cheetah Conservation Station and a cheetah research and breeding facility. The years 2004 and 2005 saw the births of cheetah litters at the zoo. At the St. Louis Zoo in Missouri, more than 30 cheetahs have been born since 1974.

In Namibia, where 20 percent of the world's cheetah population is located, scientists study cheetah movements and how the cats function within their environment. Here, the cheetah's natural habitat has been largely overtaken by farmland and land needed for livestock

grazing. Ninety-five percent of Namibia's cheetahs live on farmland. Scientists monitor the range needed by cheetahs, what they eat, where they roam, and how they reproduce. Studying how cheetahs survive in this environment can help **conservationists** in other countries protect the cheetah.

Across Africa, wild cheetahs are captured, studied, and released back into the wild. Captured cheetahs are fitted with collars. The collars monitor their movements using a Global Positioning System (GPS). This helps scientists better track the cheetahs' range and population. Captured cheetahs are examined for diseases that could

*Namibia, with its approximately 2,500 cheetahs, is also home to rival farms and herds of goats.*

*Scientists can more easily track cheetahs that travel in groups and live within a reserve's boundaries.*

pose a threat to the larger cheetah population. The DNA of more than 450 wild cheetahs has been studied and recorded. This provides a valuable database of information on wild cheetahs.

Because cheetahs are **elusive** by nature, many can easily escape capture. For this reason, researchers often set up "trigger" cameras with infrared beams. When a cheetah steps through an invisible beam, the action triggers the camera, and an image is taken. Each cheetah's distinctive pattern of spots helps researchers identify and keep track of individual animals. Careful monitoring of the population helps researchers take action if there appears to be a threat to overall cheetah survival.

Smaller populations of cheetahs live in game reserves such as the Serengeti National Park in Tanzania and Masai Mara National Reserve in Kenya. Scientists at Serengeti Park conduct the world's only ongoing long-term study of wild cheetahs. First called the Serengeti Cheetah Project, it has since expanded and been renamed the Tanzania Cheetah Conservation Program. Visitors to the park can help the scientists gather valuable information by taking photographs, which are used to get a more accurate count of the cheetah population.

The Cheetah Conservation Fund (CCF), which is headquartered in Namibia, is the leading organization dedicated to cheetah research, education, and conservation. To educate people, CCF staff members travel to schools to give presentations, and they train students in ways that the children can contribute to research efforts. Students help take counts of cheetahs and their prey and are taught laboratory techniques such as studying cheetahs' blood samples. In the 1990s, the CCF also worked with students to gather stories and poems about cheetahs, compiling their work in *The Orphan Calf and the Magical Cheetah: Cheetah Poems, Essays, and Illustrations by Children of Namibia.*

To prevent the damage that was done to cheetah populations in the 1980s from happening again, the CCF began the Livestock Guarding Dog program in 1994. This program provided Anatolian shepherd dogs to Namibian farmers to protect livestock. The Anatolian shepherd dog has been bred to stay close to the livestock, and when a threat such as a cheetah appears, the dog is trained to bark. Because cheetahs are not usually aggressive, they tend to

*Cheetahs take advantage of dead, fallen trees as convenient hiding places when they need shelter.*

**Cheetahs generally display aggression only when predators threaten cubs, and males sometimes fight each other to defend territory.**

retreat from the dog without a fight. Since the program began, 80 percent of farmers have reported fewer livestock losses and, therefore, a lesser need to kill cheetahs.

The Bushblok program, which was developed in 2001 by the CCF, helps create more natural habitat for the cheetah. "Bush encroachment" occurs when thornbush, an invasive species of shrub, multiplies and overtakes cheetah habitat. Namibians are employed to harvest the bush, and the wood is used as household fuel. This helps restore cheetah habitat, and it also provides employment for Namibians. Thousands of tons of are shipped to Europe and South Africa each year.

When the cheetah population in Namibia was reduced by half in the 1980s, the future for cheetahs looked very bleak indeed. But thanks to education efforts and programs such as Bushblok and the Livestock Guarding Dog, the dangerous decline of cheetah populations no longer continues. Scientists, researchers, and those who care about the cheetah hope that these careful efforts will one day result in population increases, and that the cheetah, much beloved and revered for thousands of years, will be around for thousands more.

Conservationists hope that cheetahs will increase their numbers and not be as lonely on the open savanna.

## ANIMAL TALE: HOW THE CHEETAH GOT ITS TEAR LINES

**The following tale comes from the Zulu tribe of Africa. It gives one explanation for why the cheetah has dark streaks of fur—called tear lines—that run from the inner corners of its eyes and down both sides of its nose to its mouth. The tale serves as a reminder that it is not honorable to steal or cheat.**

One day, a lazy hunter was watching a herd of gazelles graze near a watering hole. He thought it was too hot to try to hunt them that day. Suddenly, out of the corner of his eye, he saw something move. It was a female cheetah, who was also watching the herd. The hunter watched her as she arched her back and sprang into action. She picked a gazelle that had wandered away and pounced on it.

The hunter was amazed by her speed and skill. The cheetah dragged the carcass back to a patch of tall grass. The hunter watched as three small cubs emerged from the grass to share the meal. He was struck with envy; he wished he had someone to provide him with meals. Then he thought of an idea.

"When the mother goes away for a drink tonight, I will go to the patch of grass and take one of her cubs," the hunter said to himself. "I will train it to hunt for me. With it, I can be the best hunter in the tribe. The cubs are small yet; they will not run from me. I need only one; the mother can have the other two."

Just as he had expected, the mother cheetah went away at night. The hunter sneaked over to the patch of grass, but he could not decide which cub to take.

"Maybe I should take all three," he thought. "After all, three hunters will be better than one." So he took all three of the cubs with him back to his home.

When the mother cheetah returned, she was terribly upset to find that her children were missing. She cried all day and all night. She cried so hard that her tears burned black lines down her face.

A wise old man who was walking nearby heard the crying.

"Why are you crying, cheetah?" he asked.

"I left to get a drink, and now my cubs are missing!" she wailed.

"I will find out what happened to your cubs," he told her.

The old man went to the village and told them what he had heard. One of the villagers knew that the lazy hunter had taken the cubs, for he was bragging about it. The old man became angry.

"Hunters must hunt for themselves!" he said. "It is not fair to let something else do all the work. Hunters must take pride in what they do."

The villagers agreed. They found the lazy hunter and made him return the cubs. When the mother was reunited with her babies, she was full of happiness. But the stains of her tears never went away.

The Zulu say that all cheetahs' faces are stained with tear marks to serve as a reminder that a hunter must always be honorable.

## GLOSSARY

**alter ego** – a person's secondary or alternative personality

**camouflage** – the ability to hide, due to coloring or markings that blend in with a given environment

**carcass** – the dead body of an animal

**conservationists** – people who work to preserve a natural resource or wild animal

**Crusaders** – Europeans who traveled to the Middle East from the 11th through the 13th centuries to fight the non-Christian people who lived there

**dewclaw** – a claw located on the inner side of a paw

**elusive** – difficult to seize or grasp

**encroachment** – movement into the space of another

**evolved** – gradually developed into a new form

**inbreeding** – the mating of individuals that are closely related; it can result in offspring with genetic problems

**incisors** – the front teeth that are used to cut through food

**inseminated** – placed a male's sperm and a female's eggs together in order for a baby to grow in the female's womb

**litter** – babies that are born at the same time to animals such as dogs, cats, lions, and tigers

**molars** – the teeth at the back of the mouth with a wide, flat surface that are used to grind food

**retina** – a layer or lining in the back of the eye that is sensitive to light

**retract** – to draw or pull something back in

**savanna** – a plain characterized by coarse grasses and scattered tree growth

**tuft** – an extension of feathers or hair that usually forms a ridge or fluffy ball

## SELECTED BIBLIOGRAPHY

Arnold, Caroline. *Cheetah*. New York: Morrow Junior Books, 1989.

Cheetah Conservation Fund. "Homepage." CCF. http://www.cheetah.org.

Denis-Huot, Christine, and Michel Denis-Huot. *The Cheetah: Fast as Lightning*. Watertown, Mass.: Charlesbridge, 2004.

Estigarribia, Diana. *Cheetahs*. New York: Marshall Cavendish, 2005.

MacMillan, Dianne M. *Cheetahs*. Minneapolis: Carolrhoda Books, 1997.

Wildlife Safari. "Homepage." Wildlife Safari. http://www.wildlifesafari.org/.

When a cheetah runs, the rudder-like action of its tail helps it make tight turns without falling over.

# INDEX